春節

Customs, Traditions and Landmarks |
Non-Fiction Series

Copyright © 2022 by Level Learning, INC. and Washington Yu Ying PCS™
Original and Edited Text Copyright © 2022 by Washington Yu Ying PCS™

All rights reserved. No part of this book in whole or part may be reproduced without written permission from the publisher.

Published by Level Learning, INC.

Content Contributors:
Washington Yu Ying PCS™
Level Learning - Ya-Ching Chang

Illustrations by: Josh Taira

Leveling classification based on Level Learning standard. For full description, visit www.levellearning.com

ISBN 978-1-64040-027-6
Traditional Chinese Edition

About Level Learning:

Level Learning provides a literacy focused curriculum specifically designed for K-12 Chinese as a Second Language classrooms. Our program offers 20 levels of specific and detailed objectives, leveled texts and passages, mastery-based online assessment, and analytics to enable data-driven instruction. Level Learning reading curriculum for both literature and informational text emphasize grammar and comprehension skills to help teachers develop confident and independent Chinese language readers. The non-fiction series of books are specifically designed to support our informational text course based on multiple national standards. To learn more about our entire offering, visit www.levellearning.com.

About Washington Yu Ying PCS™:

Washington Yu Ying PCS is a Mandarin English dual language immersion International Baccalaureate (IB) World school. Yu Ying's mission is to inspire and prepare young people to create a better world by challenging them to reach their full potential in a nurturing Chinese/English educational environment. Yu Ying's comprehensive IB, dual immersion curriculum equips students with global competencies for success in the real world. As a leader in immersion education, Yu Ying is determined to advance Chinese language programs and global citizenry education by helping other schools create and strengthen their Chinese programs. For more information, email: products@washingtonyuying.org

每年農曆正月初一，是中國人的傳統節日春節。中國人會怎麼慶祝春節呢？

春節前，人們會先把家裡打掃乾淨。這代表舊的一年就要過去了，新的一年要來了。

春節前,全家人會一起去買東西。人們通常會買春聯、新衣服、年糕等東西。

過春節的時候，人們把紅色的春聯貼在門上，穿上新衣服。因為在中國紅色代表吉祥和熱鬧，很多春節的東西都是紅色的。

在農曆大年三十的晚上,全家人會坐在一起吃晚飯。晚飯通常會有魚和年糕。

農曆正月初一，新的一年開始了。大人會給孩子們紅包，紅包裡有錢。錢的數字通常會有六和八，因為六代表順利，八代表發財。

新的一年到了,孩子們會放鞭炮。放鞭炮代表吉祥和熱鬧。

新的一年到了，人們會說吉祥話拜年，比如，恭喜發財，大吉大利！

二月

日	一	二	三	四	五	六
	1 二十三	2 二十四	3 二十五	4 二十六	5 二十七	6 二十八
7 二十九	8 春節	9 初二	10 初三	11 初四	12 初五	13 初六
14 初七	15 初八	16 初九	17 初十	18 十一	19 十二	20 十三
21 十四	22 十五	23 十六	24 十七	25 十八	26 十九	27 二十
28 二十一	29 二十二					

直到農曆正月十五，中國人都會慶祝新年。大家**希望**新的一年有一個好的開始。

Glossary

	Pinyin	English Definition
農曆	nóng lì	lunar calendar
傳統	chuán tǒng	tradition
節日	jié rì	festival
春節	chūn jié	Chinese New Year
慶祝	qìng zhù	to celebrate
打掃	dǎ sǎo	to sweep
乾淨	gān jìng	clean
代表	dài biǎo	to represent
舊	jiù	old or former
買	mǎi	to buy
春聯	chūn lián	spring couplet
年糕	nián gāo	rice cake
貼	tiē	to stick, to paste
吉祥	jí xiáng	auspicious, lucky
熱鬧	rè nao	lively

	Pinyin	English Definition
錢	qián	money
數字	shù zì	numbers
順利	shùn lì	smoothly, favorably
發財	fā cái	to make a fortune
鞭炮	biān pào	firecracker
拜年	bài nián	to pay a new year's visit to friends and family
恭喜發財	gōng xǐ fā cái	Wishing you a prosperous New Year!
大吉大利	dà jí dà lì	good luck and great profit
希望	xī wàng	to hope

www.ingramcontent.com/pod-product-compliance
Lightning Source LLC
Chambersburg PA
CBHW041223070526
44584CB00001B/62